owya

D1218105

ANCIENT
MESOPOTAMIA

BY TOM HEAD

Essential Library

An Imprint of Abdo Publishing | www.abdopublishing.com

ANCIENT
MESOPOTAMIA

BY TOM HEAD

CONTENT CONSULTANT

Dr. James A. Armstrong
Harvard Semitic Museum (retired)

www.abdopublishing.com

Published by Abdo Publishing, a division of ABDO, PO Box 398166, Minneapolis, Minnesota 55439. Copyright © 2015 by Abdo Consulting Group, Inc. International copyrights reserved in all countries. No part of this book may be reproduced in any form without written permission from the publisher. Essential Library™ is a trademark and logo of Abdo Publishing.

Printed in the United States of America, North Mankato, Minnesota

102014
012015

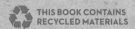

THIS BOOK CONTAINS
RECYCLED MATERIALS

Cover Photos: Shutterstock Images

Interior Photos: Shutterstock Images, 2, 12 (inset), 27, 28, 52, 78–79; Al Hoch/Janesville Gazette/AP Images, 6–7; John R. McDermott/National Geographic Society/Corbis, 9; Courtesy of Penn Museum, 10–11; iStock/Thinkstock, 12; Tina Hager/arabianEye/Getty Images, 14; SuperStock/Glow Images, 16; Stefano Bianchetti/Corbis, 19; Levgen Sosnytskyi/Shutterstock Images, 20–21; Herbert M. Herget/ National Geographic Society/Corbis, 30–31, 35, 63, 64, 77; Vladimir Korostyshevskiy/Shutterstock Images, 33; CM Dixon/Heritage Images/Glow Images, 37; iStockphoto, 40–41; Gianni Dagli Orti/ Corbis, 43, 85; Bettmann/Corbis, 45, 71; Werner Forman Archive/Glow Images, 47, 56–57, 75; Tony Baggett/iStockphoto, 49; Richard Ashworth/Robert Harding/Glow Images, 50–51; Dorling Kindersley/ Thinkstock, 54, 87; Science Source, 60; Prof. Albert T. Clay/National Geographic Society/Corbis, 67; Namir Noor-Eldeen/Pool/epa/Corbis, 72–73; The University of Chicago/AP Images, 81; Mbzt/ Wikimedia Commons, 83; US Navy, 90–91; Babak Tafreshi/National Geographic Society/Corbis, 93; Stuart Campbell/AP Images, 95

Editor: Arnold Ringstad
Series Designer: Jake Nordby

Library of Congress Control Number: 2014943879

Cataloging-in-Publication Data

Head, Tom.
 Ancient Mesopotamia / Tom Head.
  p. cm. -- (Ancient civilizations)
 ISBN 978-1-62403-541-8 (lib. bdg.)
 Includes bibliographical references and index.
 1. Iraq--Civilization--To 634--Juvenile literature. 2. Iraq--History--Juvenile literature. 3. Iraq--Social life and customs--Juvenile literature. I. Title.
 935--dc23

                                    2014943879

CONTENTS

CHAPTER 1	The First Civilization	6
CHAPTER 2	Empires of the Fertile Crescent	20
CHAPTER 3	The Lawgivers	30
CHAPTER 4	Voices of the Fertile Crescent	40
CHAPTER 5	Life in Mesopotamia	54
CHAPTER 6	Death and the Gods	62
CHAPTER 7	Agriculture and Technology	72
CHAPTER 8	Inventing War	78
CHAPTER 9	All That We Ever Were	90

TIMELINE	98
ANCIENT HISTORY	100
GLOSSARY	102
ADDITIONAL RESOURCES	104
SOURCE NOTES	106
INDEX	110
ABOUT THE AUTHOR	112

CHAPTER 1

THE FIRST CIVILIZATION

A woman named Enheduanna was one of the most powerful figures in ancient Mesopotamia. Enheduanna was still a child when her parents, King Sargon and Queen Tashlultum of Akkad, conquered Sumer and brought it under Akkadian rule, establishing the world's first empire. As Enheduanna grew older, she became history's earliest author.

The writers of ancient Akkad and Sumer used a form of writing known as cuneiform.

Her poetic works, written in approximately 2300 BCE, were the first to be credited to a specific person rather than being anonymous. This gave her an unprecedented legacy.

Historians do not know her birth name. Enheduanna was the name she took on when she became high priestess, a common practice among religious leaders to this day. Just as Pope Francis is not addressed by his birth name of Jorge Bergoglio, Enheduanna did not refer to herself by her birth name. It is unlikely we will ever know what it was.

Most of what historians know about Enheduanna comes from two sources: the text of her 47 surviving hymns and a calcite engraving called the Disk of Enheduanna. These artifacts say relatively little about her daily life or her personal history outside of the public eye, but they say a great deal about her far-reaching priorities. Her temple dedications tell us she was talented at describing gods, the communities that worshiped them, and how the two were connected.

She likely spent much of her daily life in the *giparu*, or priest's home, in the Sumerian city of Ur. Her religious duties involved rituals we now know little about. She would have probably washed and maintained the statues of the gods, overseen sacrifices, pronounced blessings, and written hymns. She also would have predicted the future, kept detailed records on the movement

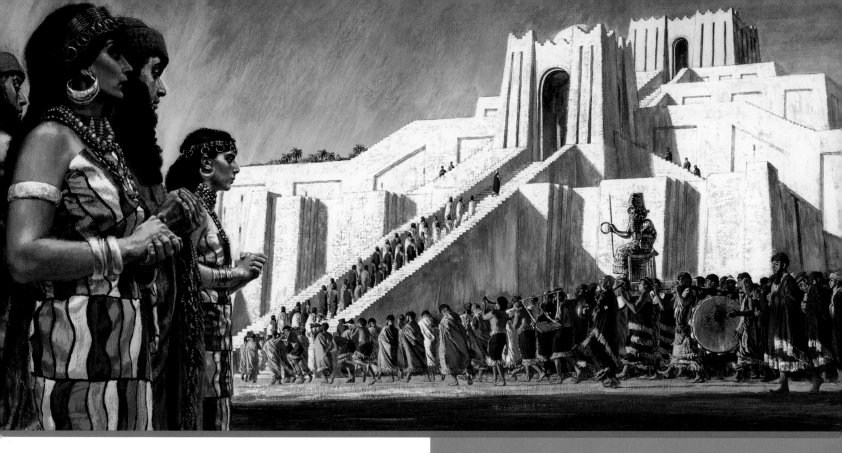

The people of Ur worshiped their gods in temples built on top of pyramid-shaped platforms called ziggurats.

of the moon and the stars, delivered public speeches, and managed the massive network of temples. These buildings were the most important social and cultural institutions of their time. As high priestess she would have also been regarded as the wife of the moon god Nanna. This made her a symbol of fertility, power, and wisdom for the entire nation.

A CLOSER LOOK

THE DISK OF ENHEDUANNA

Carved from a durable off-white mineral called calcite, the 3,000-year-old Disk of Enheduanna is approximately ten inches (25 cm) in diameter and three inches (7 cm) thick—roughly the size of an average pie.[1] Wearing an ornate headdress and textured robes, Enheduanna (*second from left*) is taller than the three other figures in the carving. Standing in front of her on the left is a naked man at what may be an altar. Standing behind her are two more plainly dressed figures whose genders are unknown. The specific context of this disk, including the exact ceremony it depicts and the role of each figure, is lost to history.

WHEN FARMERS SETTLED THE WORLD

Enheduanna's life represents a turning point in ancient Mesopotamian history. King Sargon's conquest of Sumer and the formation of the Akkadian Empire marked the transition between agricultural city-states and regional empires. Before Enheduanna was born, Mesopotamia had never been ruled by a regional power. By the time she was an adult, Mesopotamia was part of a larger empire. It would never again be made up of loosely knit agricultural city-states. Today, most of the land that was once Mesopotamia is within the

MESOPOTAMIA

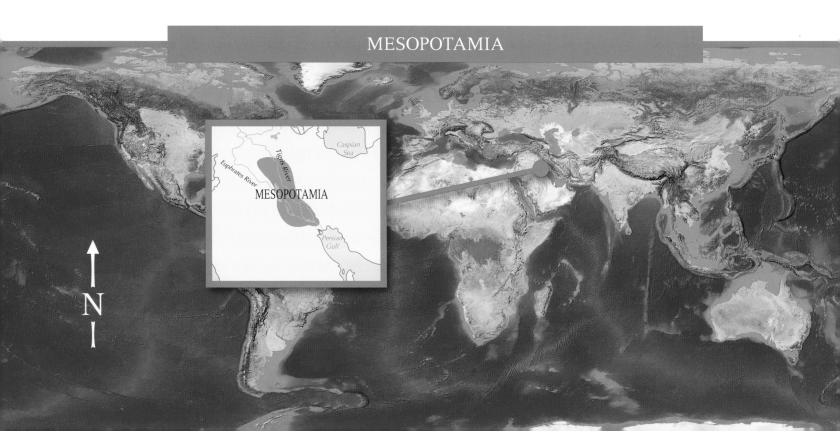

nation of Iraq, though parts of it also fall within the borders of Iran, Jordan, Kuwait, Lebanon, Syria, and Turkey.

The beginning of Mesopotamia, which was also the beginning of what we call civilization, can be traced back 7,000 years to the founding of the Sumerian city Eridu, which developed into one of the oldest known cities on Earth.[2] It was there where humanity perfected agriculture. This period was the end of the Neolithic Era, the last part of the Stone Age. The Neolithic saw the emergence of stone tools and the development of farming technology. At the end of the Neolithic Era, civilization began to consist of permanent cities rather than small, temporary settlements. Seven and one-half miles (12 km) northeast of Eridu was Ur, a second agricultural site that would soon become the cultural center of southern Mesopotamia. Other cities soon emerged in the same region. A loose collection of city-states was ruled by a single king, who—according to Sumerian mythology—was a man from Eridu named Alulim. From Alulim came a succession of many other kings and queens, and their reigns combined spanned thousands of years.

The enormous scale of ancient Mesopotamian history is hard to convey. Historians tend to think of the Sumerian period as lasting between the founding of Eridu in approximately 5400 BCE and the rise of another great city, Babylon, in approximately 1700 BCE. This is a period of 3,700 years, spanning the same amount of time as the gap between the rise of Babylon

Many ruins of ancient Mesopotamian cities are located in modern-day Iraq.

and the present day. Archaeological evidence tells us most of the first 3,700 years of recorded history took place in southern Mesopotamia in the general region of Ur and Eridu. The second 3,700 years of this history represents the entire post-Sumerian history of human civilization as we know it. So when historians talk about ancient Mesopotamia, they are talking about a vast span of time that we do not know very much about. This makes the study of ancient Mesopotamia both incredibly exciting and incredibly frustrating. It raises many fundamental historical questions about early human civilization but does not fully answer most of them.

THE GLORY OF BABYLON

As human civilization began spreading beyond southern Mesopotamia, the city of Babylon in central Mesopotamia slowly began to replace the former cities of Sumer as the area's cultural and economic center. The city had originally been founded in approximately 2290 BCE as a small Sumerian settlement. Although it continued the cultural traditions of Sumer, Babylon soon began to take on characteristics political scientists would associate with a major city today: wealth, infrastructure, cultural diversity, and a complex system of law. By the time it had reached its peak under Nebuchadnezzar II (who reigned from 605 to 562 BCE), Babylon had arguably become

Babylon in the Hebrew Bible

The Hebrew Bible, also known as the Old Testament, mentions Babylon often. The city was the wealthiest and most powerful in the region when the stories of ancient Israel were written. It is often used in the Bible as a symbol of wealth and sensuality, but other references are literal. After the army of Babylon destroyed the Jewish Temple and exiled Jerusalem's priestly class to Babylon in 587 BCE, many of the biblical texts mournfully recorded the experiences of captive immigrants. "By the rivers of Babylon," Psalm 137 begins, "there we sat down and wept, when we remembered Zion. . . . How could we sing the Lord's song in a foreign land?"[3]

Ancient Mesopotamian rulers decided how justice would be carried out in their cities. Some established complex legal codes.

Mesopotamia's first metropolis. Ur, established in approximately 3800 BCE, was important, but none of the cities of southern Mesopotamia were ever as large, diverse, or successful as Babylon.

Babylon also gave the world the most famous ancient Mesopotamian: King Hammurabi, born in approximately 1820 BCE. Hammurabi is best known for his legal code carved on stones and tablets. His code was not Mesopotamia's first. This credit may belong to another tablet, a code attributed to the king Ur-Nammu, written several hundred years earlier in approximately 2100 BCE.[4] However, Hammurabi's was certainly the most influential, and it would provide a template upon which later legal codes would improve. By the standards of today's industrialized nations, the tablet was a strange and brutal system of law if it was in fact enforced, and historians have no way of knowing whether it was. But its level of detail, sophistication, and consistency was unmatched at the time.

The world's oldest surviving work of long-form fiction, the *Epic of Gilgamesh*, was composed in Mesopotamia over a 1,100-year period. It was first transcribed in approximately 1800 BCE. The amount of time spent compiling the *Epic of Gilgamesh*, from the earliest recorded Gilgamesh stories to the first complete Akkadian manuscript, spans approximately the same amount of time as the entire

The *Epic of Gilgamesh*

The *Epic of Gilgamesh* is an epic poem chronicling the adventures of King Gilgamesh of Uruk, the brave demigod who purportedly ruled Sumer in approximately 2700 BCE and was honored as a mythologized national hero.

The epic is important because it is the oldest surviving work of long-form fiction. The story tells of Gilgamesh's corruption; his eventual redemption at the hands of his companion, the elemental force of nature Enkidu; Enkidu's decision to sacrifice his own life to protect Gilgamesh; and Gilgamesh's tiring yet ineffective effort to conquer death and learn the secrets of immortality.

history of English-language literature. No fictional character since Gilgamesh has ever enjoyed such a central place, for such a long time, in a regional literary tradition.

Although historians can only approximate the year in which the ancient Mesopotamian civilization began, it is easy to say when it ended: on October 29, 539 BCE. On that date, Cyrus the Great of Persia entered the city of Babylon and declared himself king. After 539, there would never again be an independent Mesopotamian king of Babylon. The Persians ruled Babylon until 331 BCE, when Alexander the Great of Macedonia conquered the city. In subsequent centuries, the civilization fell under the rule of the Parthians, the Romans, the Abbasid Caliphate, the Ottoman Empire, and the British Empire. By the time Iraq won its independence in 1932, the regional identity associated with Mesopotamia's ancient empires had long since been worn away by 2,500 years of foreign occupation.

The invasion of Babylon by Cyrus the Great became a popular subject of art. Later artists often depicted a fanciful version of the city.

CHAPTER 2

EMPIRES OF THE FERTILE CRESCENT

The name *Mesopotamia* comes from the Greek *mesos potamos*, "amidst two rivers," and it was applied long after these civilizations thrived. *Mesopotamia* referred to the region's location between and around the massive Tigris and Euphrates Rivers,

The Euphrates River runs for more than 1,700 miles (2,700 km), providing a valuable source of water for the region.

The Sumerian Rivers

Much like *Mesopotamia*, the names *Tigris* and *Euphrates* were later Greek terms the Sumerians themselves did not use. The Sumerians called the Tigris the *Idigina*, "fast river," because it moved quickly. More agriculturally useful was the slower-moving Euphrates, which they called the *Buranuna*, "great river."[1] Although both rivers were essential to ancient Mesopotamian civilization, most early cities were settled along the Euphrates.

the major bodies of water that determined the landscape of the ancient Near East. From their source in Turkey to their mouth in the Persian Gulf, they created moist, nutrient-rich soil and provided water to animals and plants suitable for domestication. Located at the hinge of three continents, the area was an ideal place for human civilization to begin.

The story of ancient Mesopotamian settlement begins in 6500 BCE at the beginning of what archaeologists now refer to as the Ubaid Period. The Ubaid Period gets its name from the mysterious Tell al-`Ubaid mound located on the southern Mesopotamian floodplain in the heart of Sumer, near what would become the sites of Eridu and Ur. On this site, ancient Mesopotamian subsistence farmers raised families and crops, leaving behind impressive pottery as evidence of their presence. It was little more than a campsite, though. It was not, strictly speaking, the first city in Mesopotamia.

That distinction falls to Eridu, founded in approximately 5400 BCE and generally regarded as among the oldest cities on Earth.[2] It was Eridu, along with the slightly later and ultimately more influential city-states of Uruk and Ur, that gave birth to the oldest civilization on Earth—the confederation of city-states we now refer to as Sumer.

SUMER AND AKKAD

As the southern Mesopotamian city-states united under a common language and a common culture, they began sharing a national identity. The residents of Ur, Eridu, Akkad, and nearby city-states united to govern what they called *kiengi*, "[our] native land." They referred to themselves as *sag gigga*, "black-headed people."[3] In time, kings began leading groups of city-states rather than single ones. However, it was their neighbors, the Akkadians, who gave them the name we remember them by: Sumer.

Prehistoric Settlements on the Anatolian Border

Although Eridu was among the first known cities on Earth, it was not the first known settlement. On the northern margins of the region now called Turkey lie the ruins of the mysterious Çatalhöyük dwellings, dating to approximately 7400 BCE. Deep in these ruins, archaeologists have uncovered not only practical materials, such as tools, pottery, and textiles, but also significant cultural materials including paintings and sculptures.

The Black-Headed People

The Sumerians described themselves as *sag gigga*, "black-headed people," which would seem to suggest they had the darkest physical features in south Mesopotamia. Beyond that, it is difficult to know what they looked like. There is a remote possibility that scientists may one day be able to perform DNA testing on ancient Sumerian remains to determine their physical appearance. Successful tests have been performed on human remains dating back 400,000 years.[4]

The Akkadians, a central Mesopotamian culture with their own language and traditions, united under Sargon the Great to conquer Sumer in 2334 BCE after more than 3,000 years of rule by local Sumerian city-states. The Akkadian Empire ruled over the Sumerian territory, as well as much of the surrounding land, until Sumer fell to Gutian invaders in 2154 BCE. These people came from the Zagros Mountains in what is now Iraq and Afghanistan. Few records exist of the Gutian occupation, most likely because the Gutians either had a different written language or had no written language at all.

In 2047 BCE, following a series of rebellions that overthrew the Gutian monarchy, the Sumerian king Ur-Nammu returned to power. By that time, the differences between the Sumerians and Akkadians had disappeared. Akkadian had replaced Sumerian as the primary conversational language, and the concept of an Akkadian civilization as a separate political and cultural entity, independent from Sumer, no longer existed.

BABYLON AND ASSYRIA

As the Sumerians built their civilization near the mouth of the Tigris and Euphrates, a parallel civilization began taking shape farther north. In the northeastern part of what is now Iraq, two cities dominated the landscape: Ashur, founded in approximately 2500 BCE, and Nineveh, founded in approximately 2800 BCE. Smaller settlements had emerged in the area dating back as far as 6000 BCE. Although these two city-states were initially incorporated into the Akkadian Empire, they would soon represent the seat of a new regional power named after Ashur: the Assyrian Empire.

The Gutians

Not much is known about the violent and mighty Gutians, who defeated the Akkadian Empire in 2154 BCE and fell to the final Sumerian dynasty a half century later. In surviving texts, they are generally described as barbaric and uninterested in literature, but because no surviving texts speak of the Gutian conquest from the perspective of the conquerors, it is difficult to know if this characterization was correct.

Some European scholars of the 1800s suggested the Gutians were European, citing the fact that they were sometimes described by Akkadians as *namrum*, meaning "fair-haired" or "fair-skinned." However, this theory has never been well supported by the available evidence.

Meanwhile, the political climate in southern Mesopotamia was increasingly changing because of immigration and invasion from other nearby nations. The Elamites, a civilization living to the east and southeast of Mesopotamia in what is now Iran, were particularly successful in their military efforts. They raided Ur in 2004 BCE, leaving behind a damaged, impoverished city that would never again be the center of the Mesopotamian world. The cultural focus of Mesopotamia increasingly shifted to the emerging city of Babylon, which achieved regional power as the seat of the Babylonian Empire under Hammurabi by 1750 BCE. The Babylonian and Assyrian civilizations coexisted in Mesopotamia for eight centuries, although not without occasional military conflicts.

The shape of the region changed dramatically beginning in 911 BCE. The Assyrian Empire began three centuries of military expansionism that would make it the largest empire in the history of the region. Its territory stretched as far west as Egypt, as far north as Turkey, and as far east as Iran. Conquering this territory proved easier than maintaining it, and a series of revolts led to the destruction of the Assyrian capital of Nineveh in 612 BCE and the fall of the Assyrian Empire seven years later.

The fall of the Assyrian Empire created a power vacuum, and the Babylonian Empire filled it. For nearly a century, Babylon stood tall as the world's largest city and the capital of the region's last true empire.

CITIES OF ANCIENT MESOPOTAMIA

Caspian Sea

NINEVEH

ASHUR

Tigris River

Euphrates River

N

BABYLON KISH

LAGASH

URUK

UR

ERIDU

Persian Gulf

The military conquests of Nebuchadnezzar II, who ruled the Babylonian Empire from 604 to 562 BCE, most famously included Israel. His Babylon, which conquered Israel in 587 BCE, is often referred to in the Hebrew Bible. However these conquests were overshadowed by a radical building program designed to bring about a long-term Babylonian renaissance. Nebuchadnezzar II oversaw the strengthening of Babylon's walls, renovated and enlarged his palace, and built temples. The ongoing work was interrupted when the Persian Empire under Cyrus the Great conquered Babylon in 539 BCE, crushing the last regional empire and forever ending the age of ancient Mesopotamia.

The Ishtar Gate into the city of Babylon, constructed by Nebuchadnezzar II, can now be seen in the Pergamon Museum in Berlin, Germany.

CHAPTER 3

THE LAWGIVERS

T he oldest known Sumerian documents, which can be traced back to approximately 3300 BCE, tell the story of a regional culture that had already existed for more than 2,000 years.[1] Their authors were living in what they understood to be an ancient world with ancient problems, ancient prejudices, and an ancient tradition. Historians' best guess is that those

Life in ancient Sumer often centered around each city's temple.

responsible for leading this society were its high priests and high priestesses, the most famous and influential celebrities of their era.

Living in the giparu in the middle of the city, the high priest or high priestess was seen as a spouse of the local god or goddess. This symbolic marriage represented a union between the earthly business of daily life and the unseen spiritual realms. In cities that were ruled by a high priest or priestess, this person—typically called an *ensí*—often received instructions from a council of elders. However, he or she was regarded as the ultimate local authority on both religious and secular matters. In many cases these city-states were family-oriented religious farming communities and, given their initially low population, would have most likely had a fairly informal legal system.

Historians know that at some point near 2900 BCE this changed. What historians do not know is why. Sumerian mythology tells of a great flood that forced the cities to reunite under one ruler, Etana of Kish, who was described not merely as an ensí but also a *lugal*, "king."[2] This began what historians refer to as the Sumerian Dynastic Age, in which the Sumerian city-states united as a federation under individual rulers. Later documents claimed Sumer had always had kings, dating back to the beginning of time. These were more obviously mythological figures said to have reigned for thousands of years at a time and possessed supernatural powers. The stories of their reigns might have made the transition from high priestesses to kings seem more natural and in keeping with ancient cultural traditions.

But the age of the ensí was not over. High priests and priestesses still enjoyed enormous power within their respective city-states, and a wise monarch would know to stay on their good side, at least to avoid offending the local gods.

THE CASTES OF SUMER

As significant as a transition from local, religious authority to regional, secular authority may have been, it likely had little

Images of ancient Mesopotamian kings have been preserved for thousands of years through statues.

direct relevance in the lives of most Sumerians. Local authorities continued ruling over daily business in Sumerian city-states, and it is likely most decisions were made on a case-by-case basis based on local considerations rather than broad regional public policy.

In Sumerian society the most important issue was identity, and identity was determined by caste. Ancient Sumer's caste system consisted of three tiers. The first was the *amelu*, the people who were eligible to rule. The second was the *wardu*, "slaves," who were considered property. The third was the *mushkinu*, "humble," which included laborers, farmers, and everyone else who did not belong to the first two tiers.[3] The majority of Sumerians were likely mushkinu, but most of the surviving literature deals with the amelu.

The difference between these castes was access to money and resources. It is possible that an enormously wealthy wardu or mushkinu could have bought their way into the amelu caste. In fact, it is implied that Ur-Zababa of Kish, a Sumerian brewer who became ruler, did something very similar to this. The social connections that came with being an amelu guaranteed some measure of material success. The social limitations that came with being a wardu stalled the social mobility that would have allowed someone

Huge teams of laborers were used to build and move ancient Mesopotamia's enormous stone sculptures and structures.

to become anything else. With time, and particularly after the Babylonian Empire came to power, *amelu* became a more general term used to describe free persons.

THE ORIGINS OF LAW

Ancient Babylonian civilization was a highly legalistic culture in which the Code of Hammurabi, which features the standard of justice known as "an eye for an eye," reigned supreme. Recorded in 1772 BCE and discovered by archaeologists in 1901 CE, Hammurabi's code is the part of ancient Mesopotamian culture with which most people are most familiar today.

The Code of Ur-Nammu

The Code of Ur-Nammu, who reigned between approximately 2112 and 2095 BCE, predates the Code of Hammurabi by more than 300 years, but it is not nearly as widely known. The most important reason for this is that historians have no complete text of the Code of Ur-Nammu; they have only fragments.

The text is notable primarily because it may document a changing role of women in the culture at the end of the Sumerian period. Earlier Sumerian texts suggest women were once powerful merchants, undisputed rulers of cities, and in one case even ruled the entire region, but in the code they are relegated to second-class citizenship. For example, a man who rapes his neighbor's wife pays a small fine, but a woman who has consensual sex with a married man is sentenced to death. The man receives no punishment.

Although the Code of Hammurabi is not the oldest ancient Mesopotamian legal code, its presentation as a series of engravings on a seven-foot (2.1 m) black stela is ominous enough to hint at its content. Among the laws is:

> *If a builder build a house for a man and do not make its construction firm, and the house which he has built collapse and cause the death of the owner of the house, that builder shall be put to death. If it cause the death of a son of the owner of the house, they shall put to death a son of that builder.[4]*

The Code of Hammurabi includes a total of **282** laws.

Although ancient Mesopotamian legal codes relied on the death penalty, mutilation, and fines, scholars suspect the Mesopotamian legal system was not very far-reaching. The legal code may have functioned more as a deterrent than as an actual description of how crimes were regularly punished.

Babylonian courts did not concern themselves exclusively with criminal law. A significant portion of the surviving literature of ancient Mesopotamia consists of contracts and deeds of sale. Contracts were written for loans, marriages, divorces, and many other purposes. Scribes of the ancient period served a function comparable with the one attorneys serve today. Although

The Trial by Ordeal

Ancient legal codes typically had an option to try a defendant by subjecting him or her to a life-threatening ordeal. The principle behind this method was that if the person is innocent, the gods will save him or her from death. This kind of trial is associated primarily with medieval European prosecutions of alleged witches, but the Code of Hammurabi also includes such a statute:

If a man charge a man with sorcery, and cannot prove it, he who is charged with sorcery shall go to the river, into the river he shall throw himself and if the river overcome him, his accuser shall take to himself his house. If the river show that man to be innocent and he come forth unharmed, he who charged him with sorcery shall be put to death. He who threw himself into the river shall take to himself the house of his accuser.[5]

this is partly because scribes were the most literate members of society, their authorization of ancient Mesopotamian contracts, bills of sales, and other legal documents suggest no contractual transaction could proceed without them.

The "Praise Poem of Urukagina"

That ancient Mesopotamia gave the world its first legal codes is common knowledge, but few know that it also gave the world its first human rights document. The "Praise Poem of Urukagina," written in approximately 2350 BCE, describes the city of Lagash's program of local reforms. It also defends the rights of the poor and speaks out against government corruption. Among a long list of past abuses and future promises, the surviving fragment includes this line: "Urukagina promises [his god] Ningirsu that he would never subjugate the waif and the widow to the powerful."[6] Although other documents of the time indicate Urukagina did not keep some of his promises, it is significant that he made these promises at all.

VOICES OF THE FERTILE CRESCENT

S umerian documents dating as far back as 3000 BCE have been found, but that is not where the story of the Sumerian language begins. The documents demonstrate the existence of a language that had already established a grammar and a vocabulary and

Cuneiform was used by multiple ancient Mesopotamian civilizations.

entered widespread use. It is reasonable to presume other spoken languages may have come and gone in ancient Mesopotamia in the millennia before a system of writing was developed. If they did, they are all lost to history.

Sumerian is regarded as a linguistic isolate, meaning it cannot be traced to an older language and cannot be classified into a family of languages. Its written script is known as cuneiform, meaning "wedge-shaped." The script was impressed into soft clay using styluses made from firm reeds.

When Akkadian began replacing Sumerian as the language of the people following Sargon the Great's conquest of Sumer in 2334 BCE, it bore some similarities to the old language. It, too, was a cuneiform script, and it incorporated some Sumerian words into its vocabulary. But Akkadian, unlike Sumerian, was a Semitic language. It had a clear family relationship with other languages from the same region. The language did not suggest geographic and cultural isolation as Sumerian did.

During the period of Assyrian conquest, from 911 to 605 BCE, Aramaic began replacing Akkadian as the language of Mesopotamia. Unlike Akkadian and Sumerian, Aramaic was a very widely spoken language of the region. It is perhaps best remembered today as the language spoken by Jesus Christ and his contemporaries. The transition from Akkadian to Aramaic came as the native Mesopotamian empires dissolved.

A damaged ancient copper head is believed by some to depict Sargon.

ECHOES FROM THE LYRES OF UR

By 1950 CE, French archaeologist Claude F. A. Schaeffer had been meticulously excavating a royal palace on the west coast of Syria for more than 20 years.[1] He had discovered a wealth of information about the ancient world, but there was one thing he did not expect to find: the world's oldest surviving piece of sheet music. Dubbed "Hurrian Hymn No. 6," it is written in Akkadian and features ancient Mesopotamian instruments. Scholars are still not completely sure how it might have sounded, but contemporary musicians have made multiple attempts to record the hymn using reproductions of ancient instruments.

Evidence of other Mesopotamian musical instruments suggests individuals and choruses sang accompanied by flutes, lyres, and drums. Although most of the Mesopotamian songs discovered by archaeologists are religious in character, several love songs and at least one lullaby survive.

The Lullaby of Shulgi-simti

Historians don't know much about Shulgi-simti, not even her name; *Shulgi-simti* simply means "wife of Shulgi." Shulgi was the Sumerian king of Ur from approximately 1955 BCE until 1907 BCE. Still, Shulgi-simti is widely known as the author of the world's oldest lullaby:

In my song of joy—he will grow stout,
In my song of joy—he will grow big,

Like the irina-tree he will grow stout of root,
Like the šakir-plant he will grow broad of crown. . .
My son, sleep is about to overtake you,
Sleep is about to settle on you.[2]

Future verses promise that her son will have a long life. This was a very real concern at a time in history when approximately one in three infants did not survive.

Some ancient Sumerian instruments have been reconstructed from fragments.

Archaeologists also have several actual instruments from the period. Among the most well-known artifacts from the Royal Cemetery of Ur, dating to 2450 BCE, are a silver double-flute, nine silver lyres, two harps, and cymbals. Archaeologists also found a *sistrum*, or sacred rattle, a loud percussion instrument consisting of three metal rods hooked into a bronze loop. Although it is impossible to know exactly how ancient Sumerians would have played these instruments, it is clear from their context and the craftsmanship involved that mastering each involved considerable practice.

ART AND ARCHITECTURE

From ornate and sophisticated royal tombs to murals, pottery, and minimalist carvings, the city-states of Sumer were bright and gloriously visual. Even clay seals and tablets—although they were legible only to scribes—look like works of art. This love of textured surfaces also carried over to buildings; walls were often marked or engraved, sometimes ornately so. Whatever else can be said of ancient Sumer, Akkad, Assyria, and Babylon, all of these civilizations produced beautiful art.

The most impressive architectural achievements of ancient Mesopotamia were the squared multilevel pyramids called ziggurats. The term *ziggurat* comes from the Sumerian *ziqquratu*, "built on a high place." The squared multilevel structures feature massive, ornate steps and a temple sanctuary at the pinnacle. The most impressive of these was Babylon's Etemenanki, "House of the Bond between Heaven and Earth."

Images and writing often went hand in hand in ancient Mesopotamian art.

FROM EARTH TO SKY

Although they were not generally regarded as monument builders on the scale of the ancient Egyptians, the architects of Sumer, Akkad, Assyria, and Babylonia were among the most accomplished of the ancient world.

A CLOSER LOOK

THE GREAT ZIGGURAT OF UR

The massive Great Ziggurat of Ur was not the largest in Mesopotamia. That distinction probably fell to the Etemenanki, the Great Ziggurat of Babylon. Still, it was certainly among the most intimidating. The base of the structure measures 210 feet (64 m) by 150 feet (46 m), and it stands

approximately 50 feet (15 m) tall. Three of the sides feature steep walls rising from the ground. The fourth side has three 70-foot (21 m) staircases intersecting at a gate at the top. Each has 100 steps.[3] Above this is another staircase leading to a small temple in which the high priestess worked and received instruction from the moon god Nanna.

Built by Ur-Nammu in approximately 2100 BCE, it was restored 1,400 years later by Babylonian rulers eager to display the wealth and power of Babylon.

The Tower of Babel was imagined by later artists as an impossibly grand structure.

Because their monuments were not as well preserved as those of Egypt, they remain relatively mysterious to us. Two of the most mysterious are also the most famous examples: the Tower of Babel and the Hanging Gardens of Babylon.

Historians and archaeologists have typically associated the story of the Tower of Babel with the Etemenanki, the Great Ziggurat of Babylon.

This ziggurat had been damaged in war and was under renovation at the time the Jewish religious community was exiled to Babylon in 587 BCE. It is mentioned in the Hebrew Bible.

The Hanging Gardens of Babylon are more mysterious. Although classified as one of the Seven Wonders of the Ancient World, they remain frustratingly elusive to historians today, even though ancient historians seemed to be casually familiar with them.

One of these historians was the Babylonian priest and astrologer Berosus. He was in touch with the ancient traditions of his people, but he also communicated well in the Greek language of the Macedonian Empire that ruled over Babylon during his lifetime. He put both strengths to work in his short masterpiece *Babyloniaca*, written in 290 BCE. In the work, he explained the Babylonian world to the Greeks. Much of what he wrote has been verified by archaeologists, but there was one wonder he described that has not been found: the Hanging Gardens of Babylon, which he attributed to Nebuchadnezzar II.

Berosus's own description of the gardens was fairly modest: "[Nebuchadnezzar] adorned his palace with trees, naming it the Hanging Garden."[4] This may have simply been Etemenanki, which was partially destroyed by Alexander the Great in 323 BCE and could plausibly have

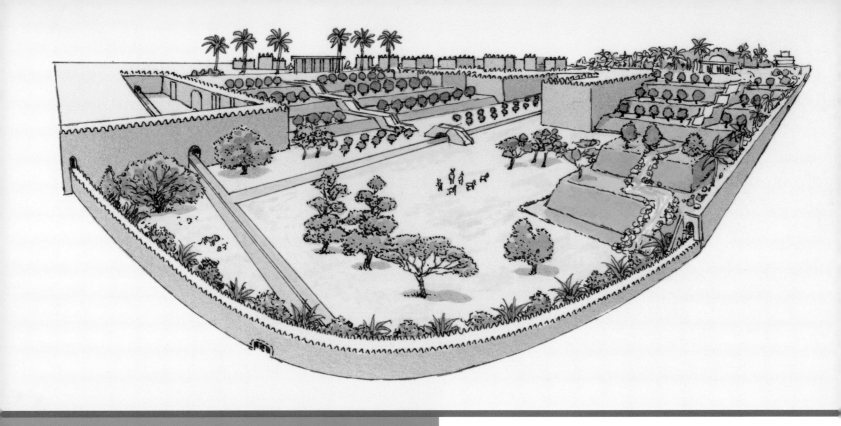

No trace of the Hanging Gardens of Babylon has been found, leaving historians and artists to guess at their true nature.

functioned as garden ruins for decades to come. However, the accounts of later historians were much more specific and ruled out the possibility that the Hanging Gardens were at Etemenanki. The Greek philosopher Strabo, who lived between 62 BCE and 24 CE, gave the most specific description, although it is not clear he verified it firsthand:

The garden is quadrangular in shape, and each side is [404 feet (122 m)] in length. It consists of arched vaults, which are situated, one after another, on checkered, cube-like foundations. The checkered foundations, which are hollowed out, are covered so deep with earth that they admit of the largest of trees, having been constructed of baked brick and asphalt—the foundations themselves and the vaults and the arches. The ascent to the uppermost terrace-roofs is made by a stairway; and alongside these stairs there were screws, through which the water was continually conducted up into the garden from the Euphrates by those appointed for this purpose. For the river, a stadium [approximately 600 feet (180 m)] in width, flows through the middle of the city; and the garden is on the bank of the river.[5]

Archaeologists and historians have been unable to find evidence of the Hanging Gardens' location, or even tangible evidence of their existence.

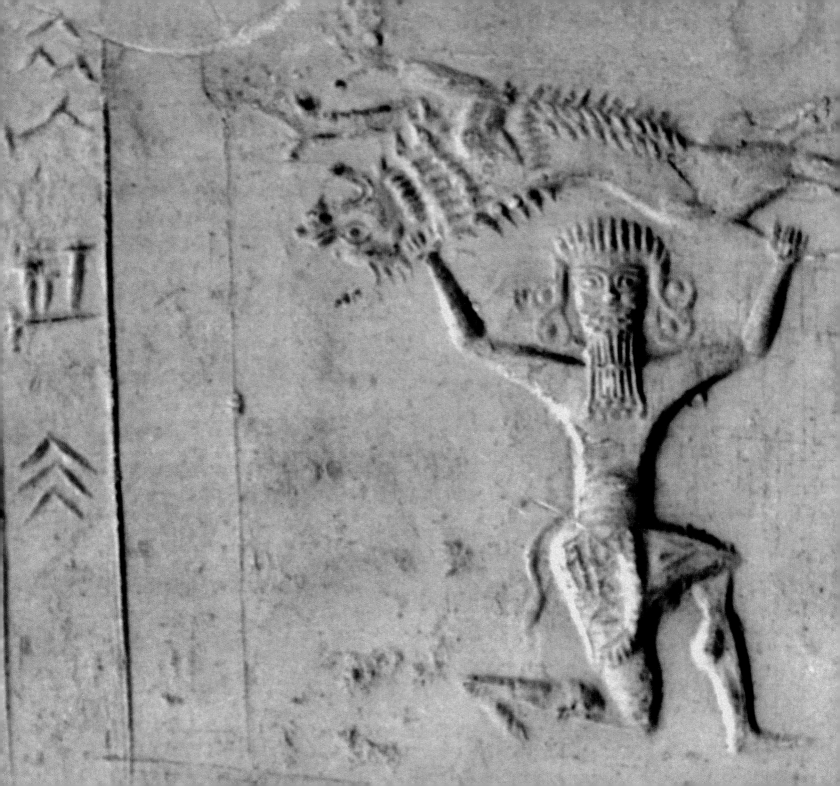

CHAPTER 5

LIFE IN MESOPOTAMIA

Residents of the oldest civilization in human history were surrounded by music and chants, savory roasts and rich candy, incense and aromatic herbs, brightly colored clothing and glistening skin, and looming architecture and distinctive houses. The stories of their time dealt with the same realities as the stories from today: life and death, love and

The presence of the hero Gilgamesh in Mesopotamian literature and art demonstrates the story's importance to the ancient people.

despair, violence and restoration, and shame and glory. These stories and their heroes provided a cultural backdrop that set the tone for daily life in ancient Mesopotamia.

SUNRISE IN UR

In 2030 BCE, Ur was in its prime. After centuries of Akkadian and Gutian rule, it was back in Sumerian hands under the authority of Ur-Nammu. His program of reforms included a written code of law and the completion of Ur's massive Great Ziggurat, which loomed over the city like a sacred fortress. The population of the city had reached its peak at approximately 65,000 residents.[1] A silver currency system of shekels, minas, and talents had begun, and the economy was thriving. The common language had recently transitioned from Sumerian to Akkadian, but most prayers and texts were still written in Sumerian. It is likely many adult residents of the city spoke both languages to some degree.

Morning for a mushkinu, a middle-class Sumerian, generally began with waking up on a reed mattress on the house's open second story, if the weather was warm. People descended the stairs to say morning prayers and eat some barley flatbread for breakfast, along with some honey and dates if they were in supply. Most residents had drinkable water, soap, and oils for personal hygiene. Both women and men combed and styled their hair. Men were also expected to comb and style their beards, and women were often expected to wear a head covering. Clothing for both sexes consisted of a skirt, sandals, a wool tunic, and distinctive jewelry. Then it was off to work. Most mushkinu were farmers. Others worked as potters, tailors, stonemasons, brewers, or in other skilled trades. After a hard day's work, a Babylonian might eat a grain cake cooked with dates or some other fruit, along with dried fish and a pitcher of beer.

AFTERNOON IN NINEVEH

By 650 BCE, the Assyrian Empire was the dominant power in Mesopotamia. The Sumerian and Akkadian nations were no more, and Babylon was under Assyrian occupation. This was good news for residents of the new Assyrian capital of Nineveh. Although it had been continuously occupied since the area was first settled in 6000 BCE, Nineveh was essentially rebuilt by the mighty kings Sennacherib and Ashurbanipal in the 600s BCE to serve as the empire's nucleus and their own home base. Among its many unique attractions was

Mesopotamian Fruit

Ancient Mesopotamian civilizations grew a wide range of foods, but one of the staple foods was the date, which is still very popular in the region to this day. Dates and date syrup made bitter grain cereals palatable, added variety to what could sometimes be a bland diet, contributed calcium and iron to a diet that was sometimes low in both, provided a quick burst of carbohydrate energy, and were an excellent source of fiber.

the world's first library, which included approximately 30,000 volumes.[2] In its prime, Nineveh was a global center of intellectual life.

Nineveh was also a very traditional Mesopotamian city in some ways. The basic morning routine someone might have had in Ur in 2030 BCE would still apply to most working-class people in Nineveh. The prayers might be said to different gods, the flatbread might be eaten with date syrup instead of honey, and the tunic might even be cotton instead of wool, but there were no dramatic shifts in daily life in a span of more than 1,000 years. Aramaic had gradually begun to replace Akkadian as the language of the people, and Sumerian had fallen further into the background, but Ashurbanipal himself claimed to read, write, and speak all three languages.

SUNSET IN BABYLON

By 560 BCE, ancient Mesopotamia was approaching its end. Assyria had fallen, and Babylonia had risen once more to become more powerful than ever. Yet in only 21 years, the Persians would crush the

A damaged tablet depicting ancient constellations was among the writings found in the ruins of Nineveh's famous library.

The Land of Beer

Beer, and particularly beer made by fermenting twice-baked *bappir*, a kind of barley bread, was the unofficial national drink of ancient Mesopotamia.[3] Every city had its own specialty artisan beers, and the best brewers were respected as minor celebrities of their time. One, Kubaba of Kish, even ended up as king of Sumer. Wine, although also widely consumed in ancient Mesopotamia, was not as popular.

Babylonian Empire, seize Babylon, and become the first of many long-term regional occupiers. An indigenous Mesopotamian empire would never again take the world stage. Akkadian and Sumerian would gradually fall out of use, replaced completely by Aramaic. Persian, Greek, and Roman influences would eradicate the everyday routine of the ancient Mesopotamian world. Even the traditional religions would gradually fall away as imperial colonists and missionaries from other faiths pushed out the old ways.

By traditional measurements, the Babylon of 560 BCE did not look like the capital of an empire in decline. The 300-foot (91 m) Etemenanki dominated a Babylonian landscape that was walled, densely populated, and eight miles (13 km) wide. With 200,000 people spread out over more than 2,000 acres (800 ha) of land, it was undeniably the largest and most powerful city on Earth.[4] But it would not remain so for long.

The Babylonian Clock

The units of time in use in the contemporary world were invented in Babylon. The Babylonian year consisted of 12 months; the Sumerian week, 7 days; the Babylonian day, 24 hours; the Babylonian hour, 60 minutes; and the Babylonian minute, 60 seconds.[5] The only major difference from today was that Babylon used a lunar calendar. This type of calendar follows the phases of the moon. A complete lunar cycle lasts approximately 29.5 days. The most common system today is a solar calendar, in which one year corresponds to one revolution of Earth around the sun.

The enormous walls and gates of Babylon defended it against competing cities and armies.

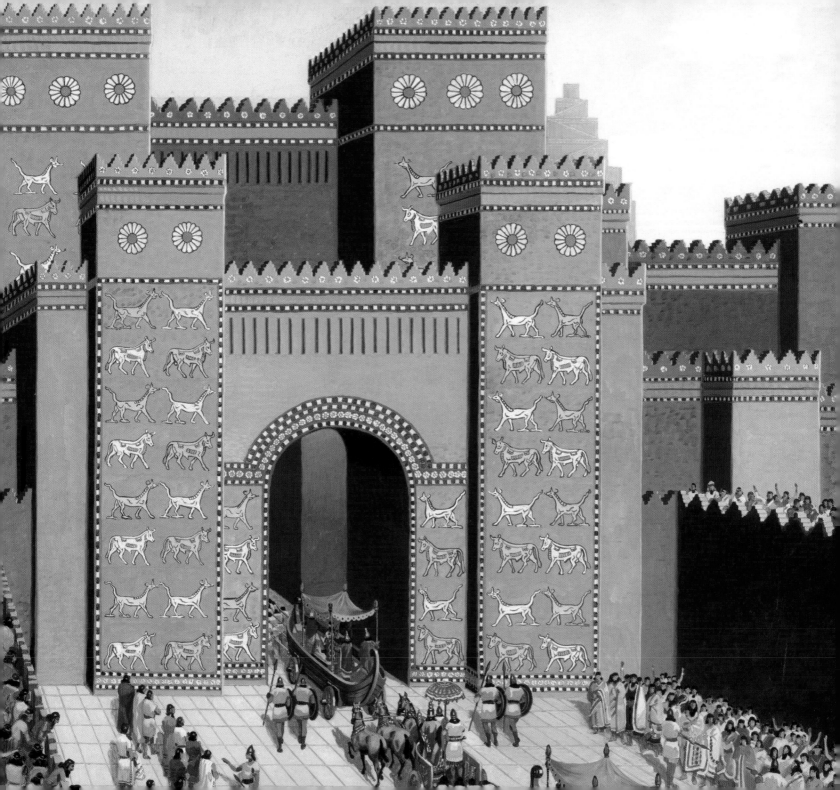

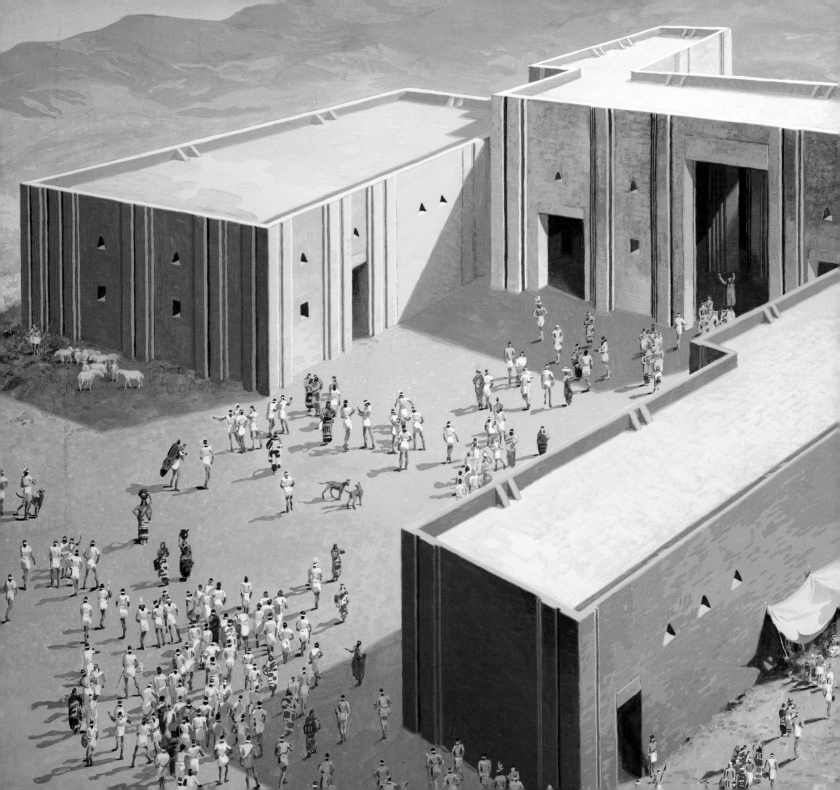

CHAPTER 6

DEATH AND THE GODS

In Sumerian religion, as in Sumerian politics, Eridu was the beginning of all things. The Sumerian creation story tells how Eridu was founded by the gods when humanity was created. It also tells how Eridu's patron god, Enki, later saved humanity from a global flood. The primacy of Eridu and Enki would not last forever. The gradual transition toward an emphasis on

Ancient Mesopotamians typically worshiped gods specific to their own city in their temples.

Babylon and the god Marduk in religious stories mirrored the political shift toward Babylon in the region as a whole.

When cities achieved political dominance, their gods took on new powers. When cities vanished, their gods often diminished as well. It is no coincidence, for example, that Ashur, the patron god of the city of the same name, was worshiped as the supreme god of the region when Ashur became the seat of the emerging Assyrian Empire. For similar reasons, Marduk, associated historically with the leadership of Babylon, achieved primary status in the Mesopotamian pantheon when the Babylonian Empire rose to power.

What this amounted to was a kind of political religion, in which power among the gods clearly and openly reflected power on Earth. It was common to interpret worldly success as evidence of a god's intervention. If a city became more powerful, its residents would logically credit the patron god or goddess and insist he or she be appropriately represented in religious texts. Mesopotamian traditions also had a tendency to absorb neighboring deities into their religions rather than competing with them, which probably contributed to peace in the region.

As a result of these phenomena, contemporary historians looking back on ancient Mesopotamian religious texts will find a wide range of contradictory

Large temples have been excavated throughout Mesopotamia.

stories in three languages with multiple overlapping pantheons. This characteristic makes the study of ancient Mesopotamian religion both difficult and fascinating. In addition, new texts are always being discovered, and new translations shed fresh light on stories scholars thought they already understood. Nobody today completely understands Mesopotamian religion, and that is one of the most exciting things about it.

A CLOSER LOOK

THE TOMB OF PUABI

British archaeologist Leonard Woolley uncovered the tomb of Puabi in 1928 CE. Puabi died in Ur at some point near 2600 BCE at approximately age 40. She was of Akkadian ancestry, which historians believe would have been relatively rare in Sumer at that time. She was slightly less than five feet (1.5 m) tall.[1] She was a person of significance who had titles of nobility and was buried in a royal tomb with ornate jewelry and other objects of value. And perhaps most significantly, she was buried with 15 servants, all of whom were killed by blunt force trauma to the head. Archaeologists often presume they were killed to serve as her entourage in the afterlife, but this is conjecture. What archaeologists do not know about Puabi is more striking. Was she an actual ruler? A priestess? Some other figure of importance? Nobody knows for certain.

LIVES OF FAITH

Ancient Mesopotamian religious traditions were highly visual, literary, complex, and evocative, and many characteristics of later religions were at one time associated with Mesopotamia. The political process that continuously pushed one god or another to a supreme position hinted at the monotheistic religions that would later dominate the region. The buildings and public charity works by Mesopotamia's priestly class in service of the gods impressed on the local community the power of their religion.

Surviving texts and architecture, ranging from the first religious icons of Eridu in 5400 BCE to a statue of Marduk, to whom the Babylonians looked for protection in 539 BCE, suggest the primary concerns of the people of Mesopotamia were religious ones. They had religious fears and obligations, but they also felt gratitude for the good lives so many felt themselves fortunate to lead. The temple inscription of Mari, a Sumerian city located in what is now Syria, reads, "Shamash [is] the shepherd of all the black-headed, the famous god, judge of everything endowed with life, agreeable to supplication, ready to listen to vows, to accept prayers, who gives to those who worship him a long-lasting life of happiness."[2]

GENDER AND THE PRIESTHOOD

Women in ancient Mesopotamia had several paths to social power that did not center on marriage. One was through trade. Brewers, in particular, were usually women and had considerable wealth, autonomy, and influence. One brewer, Kubaba, even became ruler of Sumer—the only woman recorded to have such power. But the majority of powerful women mentioned in ancient texts were priestesses, and they frequently ruled city-states as ensí whose social and economic power exceeded that of all but the most powerful men.

The priesthood also offered sanctuary for lesbian, gay, bisexual, and transgender Mesopotamians. Homosexuality in general was not socially unacceptable in ancient Mesopotamia. No Sumerian, Akkadian, or Babylonian legal code condemns it, and even Gilgamesh and Hammurabi were said to have had sexual relationships with other men. Still, the householder's life presumed marriage and a family. The priesthood was an alternative in which lesbian

The Gidim

In Mesopotamian tradition, the dead pass away and their *gidim*, or ghosts, typically move on to Irkalla, the underworld. If the gidim of the dead are forced to stay behind to wander the earth, they are not happy about it and have to be supplicated with offerings or they will cause trouble. The gidim were frequently blamed for illness. In particular, one common Mesopotamian disease was referred to as *shu gidimma*, "hand of a ghost."[3] The exact symptoms of this disease are not yet known.

and gay Mesopotamians could spend the rest of their lives in the company of same-sex partners.

And for transgender Mesopotamians, the priesthood offered opportunities to escape assigned gender roles. Particularly notable for this was the priesthood of Inanna, which featured several orders specifically intended for transgender priests.

THE MESOPOTAMIAN UNIVERSES

The world's first civilization did not have access to telescopes, large sailing ships, or any of the technologies that brought subsequent generations to a scientifically based understanding of the universe. Yet the Sumerian worldview of 5,000 years ago is based on a fundamentally accurate premise—that the world on which humans live is floating in a hospitable bubble in a massive and inhospitable cosmos. Their more specific views were less accurate. They saw the Earth as flat and covered by a dome, rather than round and covered by an atmosphere. They saw the inhospitable cosmos as a sea rather than a vacuum. Still, it is remarkable how much the ancient Mesopotamians got right by today's standards.

The Mesopotamian creation narratives changed with time. In the oldest recorded Sumerian account, a pantheon of gods created humans for labor, giving them Eridu to live in. The gods grew displeased with the humans,

The ancient Babylonians saw their world as being surrounded by a great sea.

killing most of them with a global flood but allowing others to live. In the later Babylonian tradition, the universe was created when Tiamat—the mother of the gods, and the embodiment of primal chaos—attempted to slay her children before she was torn apart by Marduk. Her body formed the heavens and earth. Both accounts represent early attempts to grapple with a complex universe that was largely beyond ancient comprehension.

AGRICULTURE AND TECHNOLOGY

Agriculture and war have always been driving forces behind technological change, and this was particularly true in ancient Mesopotamia. The prospect of settling into cities only to starve, or building thriving cities only to lose them to invaders,

The Tigris and Euphrates have enabled people to practice agriculture in Mesopotamia for thousands of years.

was horrifying enough to drive technological advancement in the ancient world. Those are reasonable fears for almost any nation, and the ancient civilizations of Mesopotamia were no exception.

The single greatest agricultural contribution of Sumerian culture was irrigation, the manual modification of the land to create channels of water, distributing it over a wide terrain and making it possible to grow crops in what would otherwise be unmanageably dry land. This invention made possible the existence of urban life in ancient Mesopotamia. Similarly, it was the building of walls—usually made of mud brick or the mineral gypsum— that shaped ancient Sumerian cities and helped transform them from temporary settlements into permanent communities.

THE ANIMAL ECONOMY

Animals were key to life in ancient Mesopotamia and were related to cultural advances, including agriculture and hunting. What has been described as evidence of human intelligence or technological achievement often turns out to be evidence of collaboration with other species. For example, a study has found that prehistoric humans became effective hunters not only because they invented projectile weapons, but also because dogs helped them find prey and protect their kills.

Animals, critical to Mesopotamian societies, are often depicted in ancient Mesopotamian art.

In Sumer, at the dawn of intensive agriculture, domesticated livestock played a similarly essential role. Oxen, the heavy-duty agricultural machinery of their era, were necessary to plow fields. Goats provided milk, butter, and cheese. Sheep provided wool. Virtually any available creatures provided food, leather or fur, bone tools and trinkets, and manure, which provided both fertilizer and cooking fuel.

STUDYING THE SKY

The Babylonians developed an advanced system of astronomy that used mathematics to accurately predict the motions of the sun and moon. This made it possible for them to establish their lunar calendar. A combination of observations and mathematics also allowed astronomers to predict future events, such as eclipses or the appearance of planets in the night sky.

However, the evidence suggests their interest in astronomy was strictly limited to religious purposes. They were interested in predicting events because of the event's potential impact on human fates. Unlike the ancient Greeks, the Babylonians were not interested in using their data to determine the physical structure of their universe.

THE FIRST URBAN COMMUNITIES

One of ancient Mesopotamia's greatest technological accomplishments is its status as home to the first civilizations. Other settlements came before those in Sumer. Even within the general area of Mesopotamia, several Turkish villages predate the city-state of Eridu by thousands of years. But it was in the permanent structures of city-states

The Power of Clay

The two most significant inventions associated with ancient Sumer were permanent cities and written language. Neither would have been possible, in the form Sumer produced them, without clay. Sumer's cities were built with clay bricks, and Sumerian writing was distributed on clay tablets. Clay has properties that still make it useful today. It is soft enough to be easily shaped, but it can be baked into a permanent ceramic that is both strong enough to support city walls and durable enough to hold its shape for thousands of years.

The development of safe, stable cities led to technological and cultural developments.

such as Eridu, and the permanent social identities they represented, that archaeologists found evidence of civilization. Advanced city-states were products of investment in the land and attempts to create permanence within it. Settling in one place provided the time, safety, and resources needed to develop new technological innovations to improve life.

There had been temples, housing, and agriculture before Eridu. But putting all of these elements together in the same city, surrounding it with walls, and filling it with streets, markets, public accommodations, and written records are what created the first city—and with it the first recognizable civilization.

CHAPTER 8

INVENTING WAR

The ancient Sumerians developed the first modern civilization with permanent cities. Soon after cities arose, people began to clash over the ownership of territory and resources. Small-scale battles between tribes had happened before, but ancient Mesopotamia saw the birth of modern organized warfare.

The development of the first professional soldiers was among ancient Mesopotamia's lasting legacies.

The earliest known weapons of the Sumerians were the spear and bow. However, enemy forces eventually developed defenses against these armaments. This led to the creation of more effective weapons, which in turn led to further defensive research. An ancient Mesopotamian arms race drove the invention of new weapons of war. The innovations of ancient Sumer included helmets, personal body armor, war axes, primitive chariots, and the first professional warriors. An enormous amount of evidence for the early history of warfare comes from a monument erected in 2525 BCE. It is known as the Stela of the Vultures.

THE STELA OF THE VULTURES

The clash in 2525 BCE was between the Sumerian cities of Lagash and Umma. Lagash, the victorious side, built the Stela of the Vultures to commemorate the conflict. The stela is the earliest record of a war in human history. It features carvings of a battle scene, giving historians a glimpse into the weapons, armor, and tactics of the ancient Sumerian world.

The weapons depicted on the stela include the socketed bronze axe and the sickle sword. Earlier axe heads had been attached to handles using leather straps. This made them prone to loosening or breaking apart.

The Stela of the Vultures is named for its images of vultures picking apart the bodies of the losing warriors.

81

Socketed axe heads were held in place with rivets inside sockets in the wooden handle. This made them much tougher. Sickle swords were even more durable, although they could not strike as hard a blow as the heavy axes. The swords were designed primarily for slashing, and they proved extremely effective. They were used in Mesopotamia for more than 1,000 years.[1] On the Stela of the Vultures, the king of Lagash is depicted multiple times, in one case holding a socketed axe and in another case holding a sickle sword.

Defensive equipment seen on the stela includes helmets and armor. Ancient Sumerian warriors wore helmets made of copper that shielded their ears and the back of their necks. Soft leather caps were worn beneath the helmets. Helmets have been discovered at archaeological sites, but the evidence for Sumerian body armor comes largely from ancient artwork. Many soldiers donned capes made of leather studded with circular bronze or copper plates. Others were much more lightly armored, wearing only helmets and sheepskin kilts.

Another invention of war found on the Stela of the Vultures is the battle cart. This precursor to the chariot had four wheels and was drawn by four onagers, animals related to horses and donkeys. Two soldiers rode on the cart. One steered the vehicle while the other threw javelins at the enemy. Historians disagree on the role of battle carts in ancient warfare. Some

The Stela of the Vultures shows the military formations ancient armies may have used.

believe the carts may have been used to smash through enemy lines of infantry. Others think the primitive carts were more likely used to chase down retreating enemy soldiers after the battle was over.

BABYLON IN VICTORY AND DEFEAT

Although the Babylonian Empire never achieved the geographic scope of the Assyrian Empire, it is the empire with which historians tend to first associate ancient Mesopotamia. This is in part because of the cultural significance of Babylon itself. It was the largest city of its time and a major cultural center. It is also in part because the Babylonian Empire conquered ancient Israel, destroying the central Jewish temple in Jerusalem, exiling its priests, and securing an unflattering description in the Hebrew Bible. But even more than that, it is perhaps because it was the Babylonians that produced the two literary works by which most people remember ancient Mesopotamia: the Code of Hammurabi and the *Epic of Gilgamesh*.

The Babylonian Empire is remembered for three great military triumphs. The first led to the empire's establishment. Although Hammurabi is more often remembered as a lawgiver and administrator than a general, his conquests of surrounding city-states in 1763 BCE created the Babylonian Empire as a political entity, transforming Babylon from a city into the most powerful nation of the region.

The second great triumph was the reclaiming of a large golden statue of Marduk, the chief Babylonian god, from the Elamite capital of Susa in 1114 BCE. The Elamites were immensely powerful. When they raided Babylon and carried off the statue 48 years earlier, in 1162 BCE, it would have been impossible to predict that Babylon would actually be in a position to bring it back by force.

The third military victory was the Babylonian defeat of the Assyrians toward the end of the 600s BCE. The Assyrian Empire, the largest ever to rise to power in Mesopotamia, seemed indestructible, particularly once it aligned with Egypt. By allying themselves with other regional powers, the

Ancient Assyria had a wide selection of weapons of war, including siege devices used to smash enemy walls.

Babylonians were able to decisively defeat the Assyrian Empire and put an end to its regional dominance.

But more often than it is remembered for these triumphs, the Babylonian Empire is remembered for one final, crushing defeat: its fall in 539 BCE to the Persian army, led by Cyrus the Great, whose military legacy would go on to overshadow that of any Mesopotamian ruler.

THE SWORDS OF ASSYRIA

In the three centuries leading up to its final defeat in 605 BCE, Assyria conquered Mesopotamia, Egypt, and much of the surrounding area. It became by far the largest of the Mesopotamian empires. The dramatic speed and scope of its conquests secured Assyria's legacy as one of the most feared and powerful empires of the ancient world. It achieved this distinction through a mix of technology, efficiency, and intimidation.

Technologically, the Assyrians relied on iron weapons, composite bows, large cavalries composed of lancers and horse archers, and chariots. These were, by the standards of their time, state-of-the-art and deadly.

Finally, the Assyrian army was noted for its brutality. Its soldiers gruesomely slaughtered, tortured, and humiliated those who challenged their authority. Assyria's well-established history of brutality against enemy civilizations is perhaps best illustrated by its history with the Syrian city of Arpad. At some point in approximately 750 BCE, King Ashurnirari V of the Assyrians negotiated rather ominous treaty terms with the city's ruler Mati'ilu, using a lamb as illustration:

> *This spring lamb has been brought from its fold not for sacrifice, not for a banquet, not for a purchase . . . it has been brought to sanction this treaty between Ashurnirari and Mati'ilu. . . . This head is not the head of a lamb, it is the head of Mati'ilu, it is the head of his sons, his officials, and the people of his land. If Mati'ilu sins against this treaty, so may, just as the head of this spring lamb is torn off . . . the head of Mati'ilu be torn off, and [the heads of] his sons.[2]*

When Ashurnirari died in 746 BCE, Mati'ilu saw an opportunity to overthrow Assyrian rule and joined with other cities to reach that goal. The Assyrians reconquered Arpad in 740 BCE, destroyed the city, and established a new Assyrian province in its place.

This sort of cruelty had the effect of suppressing rebellions in the short term, but it also meant the Assyrian leadership was easier to fear than it was to love. After the brilliant but terrifying Ashurbanipal died in 627 BCE, regions under Assyrian control immediately, and for the most part successfully, asserted their independence. The Assyrian army, although massive, was not large enough to suppress two significant rebellions at once. It was unable to protect itself from multinational coalitions. Despite assistance from the Egyptians, the Assyrian Empire was definitively crushed by a Babylonian-Mede alliance only 22 years later at the Battle of Carchemish. It never became a global power again.

The Fall of Nineveh

In 705 BCE, Nineveh became the capital of the powerful and much-feared Assyrian Empire. The empire poured its considerable financial resources into making the city the most impressive in the world. It soon became a symbol of wealth, infrastructure, and culture, but it would remain so for less than a century. At the Battle of Nineveh in 612 BCE, the army of the Medes—a group of people who lived in what are now Iran and Turkey, and whose soldiers had long witnessed the brutality of the Assyrian Empire—broke through Nineveh's defenses. The invaders destroyed the city's temples and many of its monuments, executed the Assyrian king, and left the city in ruins. It was never rebuilt.

A CLOSER LOOK

SHOCK AND AWE IN HAMOUKAR

In a site we now know only as Tell Hamoukar, located in the northeastern part of Mesopotamia near the Syrian-Iraqi border, lie the ruins of a mysterious ancient city destroyed by war. Founded at some point near 4000 BCE, the city is too far north to be part of Sumerian civilization. Whatever its origin, it did not last for very long. In 3500 BCE, a massive invasion force mowed down the city's 10-foot (3 m) walls with more than 1,000 sling bullets and more than 100 larger clay projectiles, destroying it.[3] Sumerians later occupied what was left of Hamoukar, although it is not certain they were responsible for the initial attack. Archaeologists have excavated the walls of Tell Hamoukar, providing clues about the invasion force that seized the city.

CHAPTER 9

ALL THAT WE EVER WERE

It would be accurate to say Mesopotamia is Iraq in the sense that Iraq's national borders are close to those traditionally attributed to Mesopotamia. However, it is hard to see evidence of ancient Mesopotamian culture in contemporary Iraqi society. In the more than 2,500 years since Babylon fell to the Persians and ancient Mesopotamian civilization ended,

A series of invasions over the last two millennia have dramatically changed Babylon and its surrounding area.

91

the region has changed so significantly because of war, colonialism, and immigration that Nebuchadnezzar himself would struggle to recognize it.

Greece's Alexander the Great conquered the region in 331 BCE. Between the 100s and 600s CE, the Roman and Persian Empires fought to control it. The Persians finally won, only to be conquered by Muslim armies from Arabia in approximately 640 CE. The Ottoman Empire, based in Turkey, seized Mesopotamia in 1638. The Ottomans maintained their hold on the region until their empire collapsed at the end of World War I (1914–1918). After the war, the victorious powers carved out what is now the modern nation of Iraq and put it under British supervision. The country became independent in 1932. By the time Iraq was established, the ancient culture of Mesopotamia had largely been scrubbed away by imperial influences.

The Tigris and Euphrates still flow, of course, but most of the ancient cities have been abandoned. Although its walls still partially stand, Babylon is quite visibly a former city, not a current one. Ur, whose residents moved on almost immediately after the Persian conquest, is now an archaeological site. The surviving profile of the Great Ziggurat looms above it in the distance. Ashur remained lightly populated until 1401, when an army massacred most of the remaining inhabitants and drove out the rest. Left behind are

Many of Mesopotamia's cultural treasures can now be seen in museums.

an impressive group of ruins, the most distinctive among them a massive ziggurat and the Royal Gate. The ruins of Uruk remained occupied until approximately 700 CE. They were rediscovered by archaeologists more than 1,000 years later. The ruins of Akkad, though their general location can be determined from historical records, have not been found. When they are discovered, they will likely tell us things about ancient Mesopotamian life we do not yet know.

But it is not only the cities that have suffered the effects of time. These changes have also been reflected in the less durable fabric of the nation's culture. In 539 BCE, residents spoke Aramaic, Akkadian, and Sumerian. Today, Iraqis mainly speak Arabic and Kurdish. In 539 BCE, Babylonian paganism was the dominant religion. Now, more than 99 percent of Iraqis are Muslims.[1]

WE ARE FARMERS STILL

The story of the human experience did not begin at Sumer. Anatomically modern humans emerged 200,000 years ago, complex human cultures arose 50,000 years ago, and a settlement at what is now the city of Jericho was established more than 10,000 years ago.[2] Sumer is, relative to

Archaeologists continue to make progress in understanding ancient Mesopotamian civilizations.

these milestones, young. Eridu, which may be the oldest city in ancient Mesopotamia and is undoubtedly among the oldest discovered cities on Earth, was founded only around 5400 BCE, approximately 7,400 years ago. This suggests that the first 96 percent of human history—more than 190,000 years of it—was unrecorded and took place in a world without cities, nations, wars, or written language. Exactly what took place during that massive expanse of time is unknown, though archaeologists are hard at work filling this gap.

In the course of a few thousand years, Mesopotamian civilizations laid the groundwork for the cultures that came after—including ours. Field

Hammurabi's Legacy

Today's legal codes include concepts that date back to the Code of Hammurabi, the most well-known artifact of ancient Mesopotamia. Hammurabi's laws contain a mix of penalties intended to rehabilitate the offender or provide compensation for damage. Other elements of the code provide simple penalties intended to punish, such as the death penalty or amputation. Criminal justice systems that exist primarily to compensate victims or rehabilitate offenders are said to be based on restorative justice, whereas systems that exist primarily to punish offenders are said to be based on retributive justice. Like the Code of Hammurabi, most of today's legal codes include elements of both.

archaeologist Jane McIntosh argues the contributions of these civilizations were absolutely critical to the modern world:

> *[Ancient Mesopotamia] and more particularly Sumer, its southern part, first saw the emergence of many of the developments that transformed the world into the urban society of today. Intensive agriculture, industrial production, state-controlled religion, complex stratified society, and the city itself had their beginnings here, as did many key innovations— including writing, without which we could neither share nor preserve our cultural and technological heritage.*[3]

One of the most remarkable things about ancient Mesopotamia was that so many of these innovations happened in the same time and place. Developments such as writing, permanent cities, and farming are the underpinning of our modern society. In many ways, the people of ancient Mesopotamia, including the Sumerians, the Akkadians, and the Babylonians, invented the human world as we know it.

TIMELINE

C. 6500 BCE

The Ubaid Period, marked by evidence of significant agriculture settlement in Mesopotamia, begins.

C. 5400 BCE

Eridu, described in mythological sources as the first Sumerian city, is founded.

C. 3800 BCE

Ur, the Sumerian capital, is founded.

2334 BCE

Sargon the Great becomes king.

C. 2300 BCE

Enheduanna, high priestess of Ur, writes and distributes her temple hymns. They are the oldest literary compositions in human history to have a credited author.

C. 2290 BCE

The small Akkadian city of Babylon, which will later be rebuilt to become the largest city on Earth, is founded.

2154 BCE

The Akkadian Empire collapses under attack from Gutian invaders.

C. 2100 BCE

The Code of Ur-Nammu, the oldest surviving legal code, is recorded in writing.

2004 BCE

Ur is invaded and nearly destroyed by Elamite forces.

C. 1800 BCE

The first known copy of the *Epic of Gilgamesh*, the oldest surviving work of long-form fiction, is transcribed.

1772 BCE

The Code of Hammurabi is recorded in writing.

1763 BCE

Hammurabi conquers central and southern Mesopotamia, establishing the Babylonian Empire.

1162 BCE

Elamites conquer and raid Babylon, stealing the statue of Marduk.

C. 1114 BCE

A Babylonian army led by Nebuchadnezzar I raids the Elamite capital of Susa, reclaims the statue of Marduk, and brings it back to Babylon.

605 BCE

The Babylonian-Mede army decisively defeats the Assyrian-Egyptian army at the Battle of Carshemish, destroying the Assyrian Empire.

587 BCE

The Babylonian Empire conquers Jerusalem, destroys its temple, and exiles members of the Jewish priestly class to Babylon.

539 BCE

The Persian Empire defeats the Babylonians and conquers Babylon itself, destroying the last Mesopotamian Empire.

331 BCE

Alexander the Great conquers the Mesopotamian region.

1932 CE

Iraq, containing much of the territory of ancient Mesopotamia, becomes an independent nation.

ANCIENT HISTORY

KEY DATES

- 5400 BCE: The settlement that later became the city of Eridu was established in southern Mesopotamia.

- 2334 BCE: The world's first empire, Akkad, was founded.

- 1894 BCE: The Babylonian Empire began.

- 1365 BCE: The Assyrian Empire began.

- 539 BCE: Persia conquered Babylon, destroying the last native Mesopotamian Empire.

KEY TOOLS AND TECHNOLOGIES

- The world's oldest cities were founded in Mesopotamia.

- Mesopotamian cultures created the oldest known written language, as well as the oldest known contracts and legal codes.

- Ancient Mesopotamian cities and empires remained active through the Bronze Age and the Iron Age, developing new metalworking techniques along the way.

LANGUAGE

The Sumerian language eventually gave way to Akkadian as Akkad built its empire. Aramaic later replaced Akkadian during the Assyrian conquest.

CIVILIZATIONS AND CAPITALS

- Sumer: Ur

- Babylonian Empire: Babylon

- Assyrian Empire: Nineveh

IMPACT OF THE MESOPOTAMIAN CIVILIZATION

- The development of the world's first cities and empires led to the flourishing of these types of political entities in the ancient world.

- The religious beliefs and mythologies of the ancient Mesopotamians influenced later religions of the region.

- The *Epic of Gilgamesh* has proven to be one of the most enduring stories in all of world literature.

- The Code of Hammurabi has become among the best-known legal documents of all time.

QUOTE

"[Ancient Mesopotamia] and more particularly Sumer, its southern part, first saw the emergence of many of the developments that transformed the world into the urban society of today. Intensive agriculture, industrial production, state-controlled religion, complex stratified society, and the city itself had their beginnings here, as did many key innovations—including writing, without which we could neither share nor preserve our cultural and technological heritage."

—*Field archaeologist Jane McIntosh*

GLOSSARY

amelu
The Sumerian-Akkadian ruler/priest caste; later, the Babylonian free citizen caste.

calcite
A mineral containing calcium and carbon.

caste system
A cultural system of organization in which people are separated into different classes.

cuneiform
A style of writing that uses a stylus to make wedge-shaped markings.

demigod
A being with less power than a god but more power than a mortal person.

elusive
Difficult to understand or achieve.

floodplain
Low-lying ground near a river.

giparu

The home for priests inside a Sumerian temple.

mushkinu

The most common ancient Mesopotamian caste, incorporating all nonslave laborers and craftsmen.

pantheon

The gods of a particular mythology or religious system.

stela

An upright stone slab used to commemorate significant dates in the reign of a king or queen.

ziggurat

A multilayered pyramid temple platform used in Mesopotamia.

ADDITIONAL RESOURCES

SELECTED BIBLIOGRAPHY

Bottéro, Jean, ed.; translated by Antonia Nevill. *Everyday Life in Ancient Mesopotamia*. Baltimore, MD: Johns Hopkins UP, 2001. Print.

Harris, Rivkah. *Gender and Aging in Mesopotamia: The Gilgamesh Epic and Other Ancient Literature*. Norman, OK: U of Oklahoma P, 2000. Print.

Nissen, Hans J., and Peter Heine. *From Mesopotamia to Iraq: A Concise History*. Chicago: U of Chicago P, 2009. Print.

Pritchard, James, ed. *The Ancient Near East: An Anthology of Texts and Pictures*. Princeton, NJ: Princeton UP, 2011. Print.

Roaf, Michael. *Cultural Atlas of Mesopotamia and the Ancient Near East*. New York: Facts on File, 1990. Print.

FURTHER READINGS

Morley, Jacqueline, and David Antram (illustrator). *You Wouldn't Want to Be a Sumerian Slave!: A Life of Hard Labor You'd Rather Avoid*. New York: Franklin Watts, 2007. Print.

Nardo, Don. *The Greenhaven Encyclopedia of Ancient Mesopotamia*. Farmington Hills, MI: Greenhaven, 2006. Print.

Steele, Phillip. *Eyewitness Mesopotamia*. New York: DK, 2007. Print.

WEBSITES

To learn more about Ancient Civilizations, visit **booklinks.abdopublishing.com**. These links are routinely monitored and updated to provide the most current information available.

PLACES TO VISIT
ORIENTAL INSTITUTE MUSEUM

The University of Chicago

1155 East Fifty-Eighth Street

Chicago, IL 60637

773-702-9520

https://oi.uchicago.edu/museum-exhibits

The Oriental Institute Museum features a gallery containing Mesopotamian artifacts ranging from tens of thousands of years ago to the 600s CE. This includes a wide variety of cuneiform documents.

PENN MUSEUM

3260 South Street

Philadelphia, PA 19104

215-898-4000

http://www.penn.museum/sites/iraq

Iraq's Ancient Past: Rediscovering Ur's Royal Cemetery, a long-term exhibit maintained by the University of Pennsylvania, displays artifacts from the tomb of Puabi (who may have been a queen or priestess) and other Sumerian luminaries who were buried in Ur.

SOURCE NOTES

Chapter 1. The First Civilization

1. Brad Hafford. "Ur Digitization Project: Item of the Month, June 2012." *Penn Museum Blog*. Penn Museum, 25 June 2012. Web. 23 Sept. 2014.

2. William W. Hallo. *The World's Oldest Literature: Studies in Sumerian Belles-Lettres*. Boston, MA: Brill, 2010. Print. 540.

3. "Psalm 137." *New Revised Standard Version*. Bible Gateway, n.d. Web. 23 Sept. 2014.

4. Karen Rhea Nemet-Nejat. *Daily Life in Ancient Mesopotamia*. Westport, CT: Greenwood, 1998. Print. 26.

Chapter 2. Empires of the Fertile Crescent

1. Alexander Iliev. *Towards a Theory of Mime*. New York: Routledge, 2014. Print. 233.

2. Luc-Normand Tellier. *Urban World History: An Economic and Geographical Perspective*. Quebec: Presses de l'Université du Québec, 2009. Print. 42.

3. *The Sumerian World*. Ed. Harriet Crawford. New York: Routledge, 2013. Print. 111.

4. Karl Gruber. "Discovery of Oldest DNA Scrambles Human Origins Picture." *National Geographic Daily News*. National Geographic, 4 Dec. 2013. Web. 23 Sept. 2014.

Chapter 3. The Lawgivers

1. Fred Kleiner. *Gardner's Art Through the Ages: The Western Perspective, Volume 1.* Boston, MA: Wadsworth, 2006. Print. 18.

2. Samuel Edward Finer. *The History of Government.* New York: Oxford, 1997. Print. 114.

3. Joyce Oramel Hertzler. *The Social Thought of Ancient Civilizations.* New York: Russells, 1961. Print. 100.

4. *The Code of Hammurabi, King of Babylon.* Trans. Robert Francis Harper. Chicago: U of Chicago P, 1904. Print. 2.

5. Ibid. 3.

6. *Theory and Method in Biblical and Cuneiform Law.* Ed. Bernard M. Levinson. New York: Bloomsbury, 1994. Print. 64.

Chapter 4. Voices of the Fertile Crescent

1. Arie S. Issar and Mattanyah Zohar. *Climate Change: Environment and History of the Near East.* Jerusalem: Springer, 2007. Print. 176.

2. *The Ancient Near East: An Anthology of Texts and Pictures.* Ed. James B. Pritchard. Princeton, NJ: Princeton UP, 2011. Print. 424.

3. *International Dictionary of Historic Places: Middle East and Africa.* Chicago, IL: Fitzroy, 1996. Print. 718.

4. *The Babyloniaca of Berossus.* Trans. Stanley Meyer Burstein. Malibu, CA: Undena, 1978. Print. 27.

5. *The Geography of Strabo.* Trans. Horace Leonard Jones and John Robert Sitlington Sterret. Cambridge, MA: Harvard UP, 1960. Print. 199.

SOURCE NOTES CONTINUED

Chapter 5. Life in Mesopotamia

1. Michael Dumper and Bruce E. Stanley. *Cities of the Middle East and North Africa: A Historical Encyclopedia*. Santa Barbara, CA: ABC-CLIO, 2006. Print. 382.

2. "The Library of Ashurbanipal." *British Museum*. British Museum, n.d. Web. 23 Sept. 2014.

3. Ian Spencer Hornsey. *A History of Beer and Brewing*. Cambridge, UK: Royal Society of Chemistry, 2003. Print. 84.

4. Michael Dumper and Bruce E. Stanley. *Cities of the Middle East and North Africa: A Historical Encyclopedia*. Santa Barbara, CA: ABC-CLIO, 2006. Print. 53–55.

5. Patricia Svarney-Barnes and Thomas E. Svarney. *The Handy Math Answer Book*. Canton, MI: Visible Ink, 2006. Print. 56.

Chapter 6. Death and the Gods

1. "Queen Puabi." *Penn Museum*. Penn Museum, n.d. Web. 23 Sept. 2014.

2. *The Ancient Near East: An Anthology of Texts and Pictures*. Ed. James B. Pritchard. Princeton, NJ: Princeton UP, 2011. Print. 246–247.

3. *Disease in Babylonia*. Ed. Irving L. Finkel and Markham J. Geller. Danvers, MA: Brill, 2006. Print. 123.

Chapter 7. Agriculture and Technology

None.

Chapter 8. Inventing War

1. Mark Schwartz. "Warfare at the Dawn of History." *Ancient Warfare.* 2.5 (2008): 12–17.

2. *The Ancient Near East: An Anthology of Texts and Pictures.* Ed. James B. Pritchard. Princeton, NJ: Princeton UP, 2011. Print. 210–211.

3. William Harms. "University of Chicago-Syrian Team Finds First Evidence of Warfare in Ancient Mesopotamia." *University of Chicago News Office.* University of Chicago, 16 Dec. 2005. Web. 23 Sept. 2014.

Chapter 9. All That We Ever Were

1. "Iraq." *CIA World Factbook.* CIA, 22 June 2014. Web. 23 Sept. 2014.

2. John Bright. *A History of Israel.* Louisville, KY: Westminster John Knox, 2004. Print. 24.

3. Jane R. McIntosh. *Ancient Mesopotamia: New Perspectives.* Santa Barbara, CA: ABC-CLIO, 2005. Print. 4.

INDEX

agriculture, 12–13, 22, 73–75, 77, 97
Akkad, 7, 23, 46, 47, 94
  empire, 7, 12, 24–25, 57, 59, 69
  language, 42, 44, 29, 59, 60, 94
  people, 23–24, 46, 94
Alexander the Great, 18, 51, 92
Alulim, 13
amelu, 34, 36
animals, 74–75, 82
Aramaic, 42, 59–60, 94
architecture, 46–51, 68
armor, 80, 82
Arpad, 86–87
art, 46
Ashur, 25, 64, 92
Ashurbanipal, 57, 59, 87
Ashurnirari, 86–87
Assyrians, 25–26, 42, 57, 64, 85–89
astronomy, 75–76

Babylon, 13, 15–18, 26, 29, 64, 92
  architecture, 48–53
  clock, 60
  empire, 26, 29, 36, 60, 64
  laws, 36–39
  military, 83–85
  people, 59, 68, 97
  religion, 71, 94
beer, 57, 59
Berosus, 51

calendar, 60, 76
caste system, 34
Çatalhöyük dwellings, 23
clay, 42, 46, 76, 88
Code of Hammurabi, 17, 36–37, 38, 84, 96
Code of Ur-Nammu, 17, 36, 56
currency, 56
Cyrus the Great, 18, 29, 83

daily life, 55–60
dates, 56–57, 59
Disk of Enheduanna, 8, 10

Elamites, 26, 84
Enheduanna, 7, 8, 10, 12
Enki, 63

ensí, 32–33, 69
Epic of Gilgamesh, 17, 84
Eridu, 13, 14, 22–23, 63, 68, 70, 76–77, 96
Etana of Kish, 32
Etemenanki, 46, 48, 50, 51, 52, 60
Euphrates River, 21, 22, 25, 53, 92

food, 57–59, 75

gender, 69–70
Gilgamesh, 17–18, 69, 84
global flood, 63, 71
gods, 8–9, 32, 33, 49, 59, 63–64, 68, 70–71, 84
Great Ziggurat of Ur, 48–49, 50, 56, 92
Gutians, 24, 25, 56

Hammurabi, 16–17, 26, 36–37, 38, 69, 84, 96
Hanging Gardens of Babylon, 50–53
Hebrew Bible, 15, 29, 51, 84
high priests and priestesses, 8–9, 32–33, 49, 69–70
homosexuality, 69–70

instruments, 44–46
Iran, 13, 26, 87
Iraq, 13, 18, 24, 25, 88, 91, 92, 94
Israel, 15, 29

Kubaba of Kish, 59, 69

Lagash, 39, 80, 82
language, 23–24, 41–42, 59–60, 96
laws, 15, 17, 36–39, 56, 96
literature, 18, 25, 34, 38

Marduk, 64, 68, 71, 84
marriage, 38, 69
Mati'ilu, 86–87
military, 26, 29, 79–88
mushkinu, 34, 56–57
music, 44–45

Nebuchadnezzar II, 15, 29, 51, 92
Neolithic Era, 13
Nineveh, 25, 26, 57–59, 87

Ottoman Empire, 18, 92

Persia, 18, 29, 60, 85, 91, 92
Puabi, 66

religion, 63–65, 68–70
    gods and goddesses
        (see gods)
    politics, 64
    priests (see high priests
        and priestesses)
    texts, 68
    traditions, 68

Sargon, 7, 12, 24, 42
Schaeffer, Claude F. A., 43
Shulgi-simti, 44
Stela of the Vultures, 80–83
Sumer, 7, 12, 23–24, 46, 94, 97
    cities, 8, 13, 68, 80
    culture, 74, 75, 76
    language, 24, 42, 59–60, 94
    military, 80, 82
    mythology, 13, 32
    people, 24, 34, 56–57
    period, 13, 36
    religion, 64–65, 70
    rivers, 22
    texts, 36, 41
Syria, 13, 43, 68, 86

Tell Hamoukar, 88
temples, 8, 9, 15, 29, 46, 49, 68, 77, 83, 87
Tiamat, 71
Tigris River, 21, 22, 25, 92
Tower of Babel, 50–51
Turkey, 13, 22, 23, 26, 87, 92

Ubaid Period, 22
Ur, 8, 13, 14, 16, 22–23, 26, 48, 59, 92
Ur-Nammu, 17, 24, 36, 49, 56
Uruk, 17, 23, 94

war, 79, 80, 82–88, 92
wardu, 34
weapons, 74, 82, 88
women, 36, 56–57, 69
worldview, 70–71

ziggurats, 46, 48–49, 50–51, 56, 92, 94

ABOUT THE AUTHOR

Tom Head is author or coauthor of 28 nonfiction books on a wide range of topics, including *Conversations with Carl Sagan*, *Civil Liberties: A Beginner's Guide*, and *The Absolute Beginner's Guide to the Bible*. He has served as About.com Guide to Civil Liberties since 2006. He holds a PhD in religion and society from Edith Cowan University and is a lifelong resident of Jackson, Mississippi.